Pas de deux

THE ROYAL BALLET IN PICTURES

Leanne Benjamin, Edward Watson

Pas de deux

THE ROYAL BALLET IN PICTURES

Foreword by Monica Mason OBE

THE ROYAL BALLET

ROYAL OPERA HOUSE PUBLICATIONS
OBERON BOOKS LONDON

Alina Cojocaru,
Johan Kobborg
in *Romeo and Juliet*

First published in 2007 by the
Royal Opera House in association
with Oberon Books

Oberon Books Ltd
521 Caledonian Road
London N7 9RH
info@oberonbooks.com
www.oberonbooks.com

Compilation copyright
© Royal Opera House 2007

Photographs copyright
© the copyright holders

A catalogue record for this book is
available from the British Library.

ISBN: 978-1-84002-777-8

Front cover: Leanne Benjamin and
Carlos Acosta in *Requiem*, photograph by
Johan Persson

Back cover: Sarah Lamb and Viacheslav
Samodurov in *The Sleeping Beauty*,
photograph by Johan Persson

Design by Jeff Willis

Printed by
Antony Rowe Ltd, Chippenham.

CONTENTS

Deirdre Chapman, Johannes Stepanek
in *Sinfonietta*

FOREWORD

This book looks at the work of the Company through one element of ballet: the *pas de deux*. In most ballets the *pas de deux* (or steps for two people) is the focus or highlight of the work and, in my experience, many choreographers have begun a new work by creating the central *pas de deux* first.

Taken at the Royal Opera House over the last four years, these remarkable and beautiful photographs focus on the repertory I have chosen since becoming Director. They cover a wide range of ballets, from the 19th-century classics, through our own heritage works, to those most recently created.

I hope that these photographs will, in some way, illustrate the intangible chemistry that can exist between two dancers who have developed a relationship based on trust as well as mutually sympathetic musicality and imagination. They also capture the formality or intimacy, the artistry and sheer hard work of the dancers in both rehearsal and performance.

Monica Mason

Monica Mason OBE

October 2007

Mara Galeazzi, Thiago Soares

THE PHOTOGRAPHERS

The publishers wish to thank the three
photographers whose images are featured
in this book. They appear on the following
pages:

Bill Cooper
4, 6, 11, 12, 18, 19 (both), 24, 25 (both),
27 (top), 32 (both), 33, 55, 59, 62, 64, 74, 75,
103, 107, 109, 110, 111, 120, 124, 130, 135,
137, 139, 140, 141, 142, 143, 144, 156, 157,
160, 161, 165, 177, 179, 180, 181, 183, 184,
185, 187

Dee Conway
14, 15, 34 (both), 35 (both), 36, 37, 49,
50, 54, 65 (both), 67, 70, 71, 72 (bottom),
73, 76, 77, 78, 97, 99, 100, 102, 112, 113,
114, 117, 118, 119, 123, 126, 127, 132, 133
(both), 136, 145, 150, 151, 158, 168, 170

Johan Persson
2, 8, 10, 13, 16, 17, 20, 21, 22, 23, 26,
27 (bottom), 28, 29, 30, 31, 38, 39, 40, 41,
42, 43, 44, 45 (both), 46, 47 (both), 48 (both),
51, 52, 53, 56, 57, 58 (both), 60 (both), 61,
63 (both), 66, 68 (both), 69 (both), 72 (top),
79, 80, 81, 82, 83, 84, 85, 86, 87, 88, 89, 90,
91, 92, 93, 94, 95, 96, 98, 101, 104 (both),
105, 106, 108, 115, 116, 121 (both), 122,
125, 128, 129, 131, 134 (both), 138, 139,
146, 147, 148, 149, 152, 153, 154, 155, 159,
162, 163, 164, 166, 169, 171, 172, 173, 174,
175, 176, 178, 182, 186, endpapers (front &
back)

ACKNOWLEDGEMENTS

The publishers also wish to thank the
following people who have been instrumental
in the planning and production of this book:

Maria Bashieva, Jeanetta Laurence, Janine
Limberg, Simon Magill, Monica Mason,
Hayley Smith, John Snelson, Katie Town.

Will Hammond, James Hogan, Leo Owen,
Dan Steward.

GISELLE

Leanne Benjamin, Edward Watson

Mara Galeazzi, Viacheslav Samodurov

Mara Galeazzi, Viacheslav Samodurov

Leanne Benjamin, Edward Watson

SYMPHONIC VARIATIONS

Alina Cojocaru, Federico Bonelli
with Johan Kobborg

Sarah Lamb, Ivan Putrov

THE LESSON

Alina Cojocaru, Johan Kobborg

Alina Cojocaru, Johan Kobborg

Alina Cojocaru, Federico Bonelli

Left: Alina Cojocaru, Federico Bonelli

Right: Marianela Nuñez, Thiago Soares

Alina Cojocaru, Edward Watson

Tamara Rojo, Steven McRae

Lauren Cuthbertson, Eric Underwood

Alina Cojocaru, Edward Watson

LA FILLE MAL GARDÉE

Marianela Nuñez, Carlos Acosta

Left: Miyako Yoshida, Viacheslav Samodurov

Right: Sarah Lamb, Martin Harvey

Miyako Yoshida, Viacheslav Samodurov

Top: Roberta Marquez, Ricardo Cervera

Bottom: Alina Cojocaru, Johan Kobborg

Roberta Marquez, Viacheslav Samodurov
with Sian Murphy

Miyako Yoshida, Viacheslav Samodurov

Roberta Marquez, Viacheslav Samodurov

Belinda Hatley, Thiago Soares

PIERROT LUNAIRE

Top: Carlos Acosta, Ivan Putrov

Bottom: Deirdre Chapman, Ivan Putrov

Deirdre Chapman, Ivan Putrov

Sarah Lamb, Carlos Acosta

Left: Roberta Marquez, Ivan Putrov

Right: Sarah Lamb, Carlos Acosta

L'APRÈS MIDI D'UN FAUNE

Deirdre Chapman, Viacheslav Samodurov

Deirdre Chapman, Viacheslav Samodurov

SWAN LAKE

Tamara Rojo, Carlos Acosta

Zenaida Yanowsky, Kenneth Greve

Alina Cojocaru, Johan Kobborg

Zenaida Yanowsky, Kenneth Greve

Tamara Rojo, Carlos Acosta

Zenaida Yanowsky, Kenneth Greve

Tamara Rojo, Christopher Saunders

Tamara Rojo, Carlos Acosta

Tamara Rojo, Carlos Acosta

Left: Alina Cojocaru, Johan Kobborg

Right: Zenaida Yanowsky, Roberto Bolle

THREE SONGS TWO VOICES

Zenaida Yanowsky, Gary Avis

Zenaida Yanowsky, Gary Avis

Tamara Rojo, Johannes Stepanek

Tamara Rojo, Federico Bonelli

Leanne Benjamin, Carlos Acosta

Leanne Benjamin, Carlos Acosta

Alina Cojocaru, Thiago Soares

STRAVINSKY VIOLIN CONCERTO

Leanne Benjamin, Johan Kobborg

Leanne Benjamin, Johan Kobborg

Alexandra Ansanelli, Viacheslav Samodurov

Darcey Bussell, Edward Watson

Zenaida Yanowsky, David Makhateli

Left: Zenaida Yanowsky, David Makhateli

Right: Leanne Benjamin, Johan Kobborg

Leanne Benjamin, Johan Kobborg

Darcey Bussell, Edward Watson

Leanne Benjamin, Johan Kobborg

Alexandra Ansanelli, Viacheslav Samodurov

THAÏS PAS DE DEUX

Mara Galeazzi, Thiago Soares

Sarah Lamb, Federico Bonelli

Mara Galeazzi, Thiago Soares

A WEDDING BOUQUET

Top: Roberta Marquez, Jonathan Howells

Bottom: Tamara Rojo, Johan Kobborg

Left: Roberta Marquez, Jonathan Howells

Right: Alina Cojocaru, Johan Kobborg

Johan Kobborg, Jose Martin

Alina Cojocaru, Johan Kobborg

Top: Alina Cojocaru, Jonathan Howells

Bottom: Isabel McMeekan, Joshua Tuifua

DAPHNIS AND CHLOË

Marianela Nuñez, Federico Bonelli

Alina Cojocaru, Johan Kobborg

Alina Cojocaru, Johan Kobborg

Tamara Rojo, Carlos Acosta

Tamara Rojo, Carlos Acosta

Tamara Rojo, Carlos Acosta

Tamara Rojo, David Makhateli

DGV
DANSE À GRANDE VITESSE

Lauren Cuthbertson, Eric Underwood

Marianela Nuñez, Federico Bonelli

Darcey Bussell, Gary Avis

Darcey Bussell, Gary Avis

Leanne Benjamin, Edward Watson

Marianela Nuñez, Federico Bonelli

Deirdre Chapman, Martin Harvey

Marianela Nuñez, Federico Bonelli

Marianela Nuñez, Federico Bonelli

Leanne Benjamin, Edward Watson

Deirdre Chapman, Martin Harvey

Marianela Nuñez, Federico Bonelli

Laura Morera, Steven McRae

Marianela Nuñez, Federico Bonelli

Deirdre Chapman, Martin Harvey

Marianela Nuñez, Federico Bonelli

Laura Morera, Martin Harvey

Caroline Duprot, Federico Bonelli

Marianela Nuñez, Johannes Stepanek

Alina Cojocaru, Bennet Gartside

Alina Cojocaru, Bennet Gartside

Jaimie Tapper, David Makhateli

Alina Cojocaru, Johan Kobborg

Zenaida Yanowsky, Edward Watson

Left: Marianela Nuñez, Thiago Soares

Right: Zenaida Yanowsky, Eric Underwood

MAYERLING

Leanne Benjamin, Carlos Acosta

Mara Galeazzi, Edward Watson

Jaimie Tapper, Jonathan Cope

Mara Galeazzi, Edward Watson

LA BAYADÈRE

Darcey Bussell, Jonathan Cope

Alina Cojocaru, Johan Kobborg

Darcey Bussell, Jonathan Cope

Leanne Benjamin, Edward Watson

Isabel McMeekan, Viacheslav Samodurov

BIRTHDAY OFFERING

Jaimie Tapper, Rupert Pennefather

Jaimie Tapper, Rupert Pennefather

Jaimie Tapper, Rupert Pennefather

COPPÉLIA

Marianela Nuñez, Thiago Soares

Roberta Marquez, Viacheslav Samodurov

BALLET IMPERIAL

Alina Cojocaru, Federico Bonelli

Sarah Lamb, Ricardo Cervera

Left: Natasha Oughtred, Martin Harvey

Right: Sarah Lamb, Ricardo Cervera

Darcey Bussell, Gary Avis

Darcey Bussell, Yohei Sasaki

Laura Morera, Edward Watson

Darcey Bussell, Gary Avis

Darcey Bussell, Carlos Acosta

TCHAIKOVSKY PAS DE DEUX

Alexandra Ansanelli, Federico Bonelli

Darcey Bussell, Carlos Acosta

Zenaida Yanowsky, Federico Bonelli

Alina Cojocaru, Johan Kobborg

Alina Cojocaru, Johan Kobborg
with Peter Manning

Darcey Bussell, David Makhateli

Sarah Lamb, Gary Avis

Top: Miyako Yoshida, rehearsed by
Michael Corder

Bottom: Miyako Yoshida, Valeri Hristov

PAVANE POUR UNE INFANTE DÉFUNTE

Darcey Bussell, Jonathan Cope

Leanne Benjamin, Martin Harvey

RHAPSODY

Leanne Benjamin, Carlos Acosta

Darcey Bussell, Roberto Bolle

Alina Cojocaru, Johan Kobborg

Zenaida Yanowsky, Gary Avis

Leanne Benjamin, Federico Bonelli

Alina Cojocaru, Johan Kobborg

Zenaida Yanowsky, Kenneth Greve

Leanne Benjamin, Federico Bonelli

LA VALSE

Deirdre Chapman, David Pickering
Marianela Nuñez, David Makhateli
Isabel McMeekan, Gary Avis

Leanne Benjamin, Johannes Stepanek

Sarah Lamb, Martin Harvey

Johannes Stepanek, Steven McRae

Christina Arestis, Gary Avis

Bethany Keating, Rupert Pennefather

THE RAKE'S PROGRESS

Gillian Revie, Johan Kobborg

Miyako Yoshida, Edward Watson

Tamara Rojo, Jonathan Cope

Tamara Rojo, Jonathan Cope

Tamara Rojo, Jonathan Cope

Roberta Marquez, Ivan Putrov

Roberta Marquez, Ivan Putrov

Roberta Marquez, Valeri Hristov

Miyako Yoshida, Federico Bonelli

Lauren Cuthbertson, Edward Watson
Leanne Benjamin, Jonathan Cope
Jaimie Tapper, Valeri Hristov
Alina Cojocaru, Federico Bonelli

Jaimie Tapper, Valeri Hristov

Leanne Benjamin, Martin Harvey

Alina Cojocaru, Federico Bonelli

Sarah Lamb, Federico Bonelli

Tamara Rojo, Federico Bonelli

Alina Cojocaru, Ivan Putrov

Alina Cojocaru, Johan Kobborg

Mara Galeazzi, Edward Watson

Mara Galeazzi, Edward Watson

Mara Galeazzi, Edward Watson

Belinda Hatley, Brian Maloney
rehearsed by Alexander Agadzhanov

Tamara Rojo, Carlos Acosta
Alexandra Ansanelli

Sarah Lamb, Yohei Sasaki

Alina Cojocaru, Johan Kobborg

Sarah Lamb, Viacheslav Samodurov

Alina Cojocaru, Johan Kobborg

Lauren Cuthbertson, Federico Bonelli

Roberta Marquez, Rupert Pennefather

Sarah Lamb, Yohei Sasaki

Sarah Lamb, Viacheslav Samodurov

Tamara Rojo, Carlos Acosta

Alina Cojocaru, Johan Kobborg

Natasha Oughtred, Ricardo Cervera

Caroline Duprot, Thomas Whitehead

Tamara Rojo, Federico Bonelli

Alina Cojocaru, Johan Kobborg
Marianela Nuñez

CREATIVE CREDITS FOR THE BALLETS

AFTERNOON OF A FAUN

Music: Claude Debussy

Choreography: Jerome Robbins

Costume Designs: Irene Sharaff

Sets and original lighting: Jean Rosenthal

Lighting recreated by: Les Dickert

APOLLO

Music: Igor Stravinsky

Choreography: George Balanchine

Lighting: John B. Read

L'APRÈS MIDI D'UN FAUNE

Music: Claude Debussy

Choreography: Vaslav Nijinsky

Designs: Léon Bakst

Lighting: John B. Read

BALLET IMPERIAL

Music: Pyotr Il'yich Tchaikovsky

Choreography: George Balanchine

Original Designs: Eugene Berman
    realized by Anthony Dowell

Lighting: John B. Read

LA BAYADÈRE

Music: Ludwig Minkus

Orchestration and arrangement:
    John Lanchbery

Choreography: Natalia Makarova
    after Marius Petipa

Production conceived and directed by:
    Natalia Makarova

Costume designs: Yolanda Sonnabend

Set designs: Pier Luigi Samaritani

Lighting: John B. Read

BIRTHDAY OFFERING

Music: Alexander Glazunov
    arranged Robert Irving

Choreography: Frederick Ashton

Designs: André Levasseur

Lighting: John B. Read

CHILDREN OF ADAM

Music: Christopher Rouse

Choreography: Alastair Marriott

Designs: Adam Wiltshire

Lighting: John B. Read

CHROMA

Music: Joby Talbot and Jack White III
    New arrangement by Joby Talbot,
    orchestrated by Christopher Austin

Choreography: Wayne McGregor

Costume designs: Moritz Junge

Set designs: John Pawson

Lighting: Lucy Carter

CINDERELLA

Music: Sergey Prokofiev

Choreography: Frederick Ashton

Production: Wendy Ellis Somes

Costume designs: Christine Haworth

Set designs: Toer van Schayk

Lighting: Mark Jonathan

COPPÉLIA

Music: Léo Delibes

Choreography and Production:
    Ninette de Valois after Lev Ivanov
    and Enrico Cecchetti

Designs: Osbert Lancaster

Lighting: John B. Read

DAPHNIS AND CHLOË

Music: Maurice Ravel

Choreography: Frederick Ashton

Designs: John Craxton

Lighting: John B. Read

DEVIL'S HOLIDAY

Music: Paganini arranged by Tomassini

Choreography: Frederick Ashton

Costume designs: Allan Watkins after
    Eugene Berman

Lighting: John B. Read

DGV: DANSE À GRANDE VITESSE

Music: Michael Nyman

Choreography: Christopher Wheeldon

Designs: Jean-Marc Puissant

Lighting: Jennifer Tipton

THE DREAM

Music: Felix Mendelssohn
    Arranged by John Lanchbery
Choreography: Frederick Ashton
Designs: David Walker
Lighting: John B. Read

DUO CONCERTANT

Music: Igor Stravinsky
Choreography: George Balanchine
Original lighting: Perry Silvey
Lighting recreated by: John B. Read

ELITE SYNCOPATIONS

Music: Scott Joplin and Scott Hayden,
    Paul Pratt, James Scott,
    Joseph F. Lamb, Max Morath,
    Donald Ashwander, Robert Hampton
Choreography: Kenneth MacMillan
Designs: Ian Spurling
Lighting: John B. Read

LA FILLE MAL GARDÉE

Music: Ferdinand Herold
    freely adapted and arranged by
    John Lanchbery from the 1828
    version
Choreography: Frederick Ashton
Scenario: Jean Dauberval
Designs: Osbert Lancaster
Lighting: John B. Read

LA FIN DU JOUR

Music: Maurice Ravel
Choreography: Kenneth MacMillan
Designs: Ian Spurling
Lighting: John B. Read

THE FIREBIRD

Music: Igor Stravinsky
Choreography: Mikhail Fokine
Designs: Natalia Gontcharova

GISELLE

Music: Adolphe Adam, revised by
    Joseph Horovitz
Choreography: Marius Petipa after
    Jean Coralli and Jules Perrot
Production: Peter Wright
Designs: John Macfarlane
Original lighting: Jennifer Tipton
Lighting recreated by: Clare O'Donoghue

GLORIA

Music: Francis Poulenc
Choreography: Kenneth MacMillan
Designs: Andy Klunder
Lighting: John B. Read

HOMAGE TO THE QUEEN

Music: Malcolm Arnold
Choreography: David Bintley ('Earth'),
    Michael Corder ('Water'),
    Christopher Wheeldon ('Fire'),
    Frederick Ashton ('Air')
Designs: Peter Farmer
Lighting: John B. Read

THE LESSON

Music: Georges Delerue
    based on the play by Eugene Ionesco
Choreography: Flemming Flindt
Costume designs: Flemming Flindt,
    Tina Sander
Set designs: Flemming Flindt after
    Bernard Daydé
Lighting: Simon Bennison

MANON

Music: Jules Massenet
Orchestration and arrangement:
    Leighton Lucas with the
    collaboration of Hilda Gaunt
Choreography and Direction:
    Kenneth MacMillan
Designs: Nicholas Georgiadis
Lighting: John B. Read

MAYERLING

Music: Franz Liszt

Orchestration and arrangement:
John Lanchbery

Choreography: Kenneth MacMillan

Scenario: Gillian Freeman

Designs: Nicholas Georgiadis

Lighting: John B. Read

A MONTH IN THE COUNTRY

Music: Frédéric Chopin
arranged by John Lanchbery

Choreography: Frederick Ashton

Designs: Julia Trevelyan Oman

Lighting: William Bundy

THE NUTCRACKER

Music: Pyotr Il'yich Tchaikovsky

Choreography: Peter Wright after
Lev Ivanov

Production and Scenario: Peter Wright

Production Consultant:
Roland John Wiley

Designs: Julia Trevelyan Oman

Lighting: Mark Henderson

ONDINE

Music: Hans Werner Henze

Choreography: Frederick Ashton

Costumes and Sets from Designs by:
Lila de Nobili

Lighting: John B. Read

ONEGIN

Music: Pyotr Il'yich Tchaikovsky
Arranged and orchestrated by
Kurt-Heinz Stolze

Choreography and libretto:
John Cranko (after a verse-novel
by Alexander Sergeyevich Pushkin)

Copyright: Dieter Graefe

Designs: Jürgen Rose

Lighting: Steen Bjarke

PAVANE POUR UNE INFANTE DÉFUNTE

Music: Maurice Ravel

Choreography: Christopher Wheeldon

Designs: Bob Crowley

Lighting: John B. Read

PIERROT LUNAIRE

Music: Arnold Schoenberg

Libretto: O.E. Hartleben

Choreography: Glen Tetley

Scenario: Based on seven poems
by Albert Giraud

Designs: Rouben Ter-Arutunian

Lighting: John B. Read

POLYPHONIA

Music: György Ligeti

Choreography: Christopher Wheeldon

Designs: Holly Hynes

Lighting: Mark Stanley

THE RAKE'S PROGRESS

Music and scenario: Gavin Gordon

Choreography: Ninette De Valois

Designs: Rex Whistler after
William Hogarth

Lighting: John B. Read

REQUIEM

Music: Gabriel Fauré

Choreography: Kenneth MacMillan

Designs: Yolanda Sonnabend in
association with Peter Farley

Lighting: John B. Read

RHAPSODY

Music: Serge Rachmaninoff

Choreography: Frederick Ashton

Designs: Jessica Curtis

Lighting: Neil Austin

RITE OF SPRING

Music: Igor Stravinsky

Choreography: Kenneth MacMillan

Designs: Sidney Nolan

Lighting: John B. Read

ROMEO AND JULIET

Music: Sergey Prokofiev

Choreography: Kenneth MacMillan

Designs: Nicholas Georgiadis

Lighting: John B. Read

THE SEVEN DEADLY SINS

Music: Kurt Weill

Text: Bertolt Brecht

Choreography: Will Tuckett

Designs: Lez Brotherston

Lighting: Paule Constable

Video Designs: Leo Warner and
    Mark Grimmer for Fifty Nine
    Productions Limited

THE SLEEPING BEAUTY

Music: Pyotr Il'yich Tchaikovsky

Choreography: Marius Petipa

Additional Choreography:
    Frederick Ashton, Anthony Dowell,
    Christopher Wheeldon

Production: Monica Mason and
    Christopher Newton after
    Ninette de Valois and
    Nicholas Sergeyev

Original designs: Oliver Messel

Realization and Additional Designs:
    Peter Farmer

Lighting: Mark Jonathan

SONG OF THE EARTH

Music: Gustav Mahler
    Text from Hans Bethge's
    The Chinese Flute

Choreography: Kenneth MacMillan

Designs: Nicholas Georgiadis

Lighting: John B. Read

STRAVINSKY VIOLIN CONCERTO

Music: Igor Stravinsky

Choreography: George Balanchine

Original lighting: Ronald Bates

SWAN LAKE

Music: Pyotr Il'yich Tchaikovsky

Choreography: Marius Petipa and
    Lev Ivanov

Production: Anthony Dowell

Production Research: Roland John Wiley

Designs: Yolanda Sonnabend

Lighting: Mark Henderson

LA SYLPHIDE

Music: Herman Løvenskiold

Choreography: August Bournonville

Additional choreography: Johan Kobborg

Production: Johan Kobborg

Costume designs: Henrik Bloch

Set designs: Søren Frandsen

Lighting: Mark Jonathan

SYLVIA

Music: Léo Delibes

Choreography: Frederick Ashton

Production realization and staging:
    Christopher Newton

Original designs: Robin and
    Christopher Ironside

Additional designs (revival): Peter Farmer

Lighting: Mark Jonathan

SYMPHONIC VARIATIONS

Music: César Franck

Choreography: Frederick Ashton

Designs: Sophie Fedorovitch

Lighting: John B. Read

TANGLEWOOD

Music: Ned Rorem

Choreography: Alastair Marriott

Designs: Adam Wiltshire

Lighting: John B. Read

TCHAIKOVSKY PAS DE DEUX

Music: Pyotr Il'yich Tchaikovsky

Choreography: George Balanchine

Lighting: John B. Read

THAÏS PAS DE DEUX

Music: Jules Massenet

Choreography: Frederick Ashton

Costume designs: Anthony Dowell

THREE SONGS TWO VOICES

Music: Nigel Kennedy's interpretation
    of music by Jimi Hendrix –
    Third Stone from the Sun,
    Little Wing, *Fire*

Choreography: Christopher Bruce

Designs: Marian Bruce

Lighting: John B. Read

TOMBEAUX

Music: William Walton

Choreography: David Bintley

Designs: Jasper Conran

Lighting: John B. Read

LA VALSE

Music: Maurice Ravel

Choreography: Frederick Ashton

Designs: André Levasseur

Lighting: John B. Read

VOLUNTARIES

Music: Francis Poulenc

Choreography: Glen Tetley

Designs: Rouben Ter-Arutunian

Lighting: John B. Read

A WEDDING BOUQUET

Music: Lord Berners

Libretto: Gertrude Stein

Choreography: Frederick Ashton

Designs: Lord Berners

Lighting: John B. Read